This book belongs to

_____

This book is dedicated to my children - Mikey, Kobe, and Jojo.

Copyright © 2025 Grow Grit Press LLC. All rights reserved. No part of this book may be reproduced in any form without permission in writing from the publisher. Please send bulk order requests to info@ninjalifehacks.tv

Paperback ISBN: 979-8-89614-115-0
Hardcover ISBN: 979-8-89614-117-4
eBook ISBN: 979-8-89614-116-7

Printed and bound in the USA.
NinjaLifeHacks.tv

Ninja Life Hacks®
by Mary Nhin

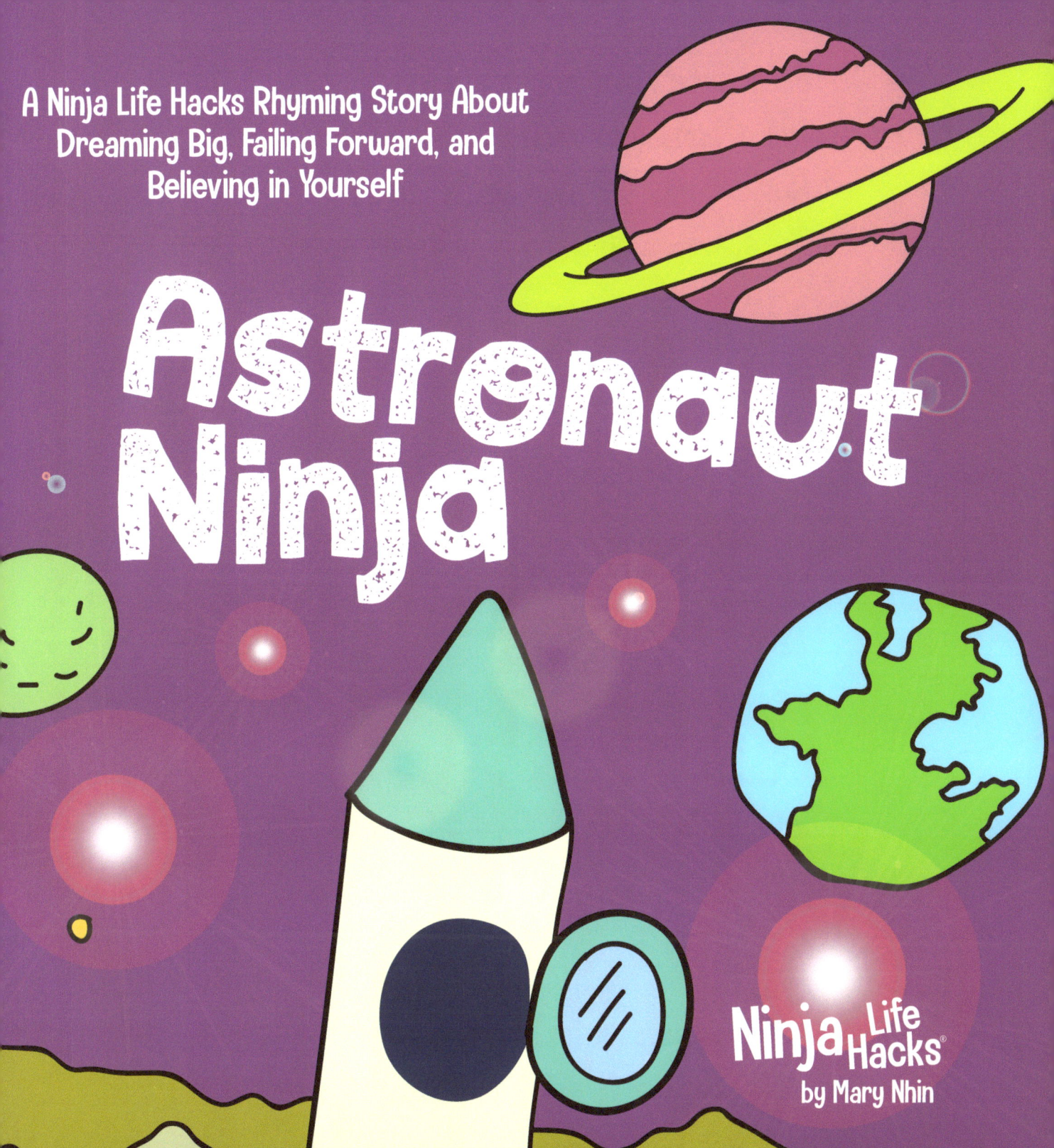

I trained to be an astronaut—
I studied hard and tried my best.
But every time I made mistakes,
my heart would sink inside my chest.

"I'm just not good enough," I sighed.
"I'll never make it past the sky."
I thought of quitting right that day,
but something deep inside said, "Just try."

So I sat down and made a plan—
a ninja hack I'd call my own.
Three simple steps to build me up
whenever fear had overgrown.

First, I pictured flying high,
with stars and planets all around.
I saw myself wave from my pod-
that dream became my solid ground.

Next, I practiced failing proud.
Each mistake became my friend.
Instead of quitting, I leaned in—
I knew I'd get there in the end.

Last, I built a goal rocket!
I wrote my dreams in bold and bright.
Then taped them to my model ship,
so they could launch into the night.

I missed, I fell, I spun off track—
but every try helped me improve.
I taped up cracks and tried again,
and slowly found my ninja groove.

Test day came—I felt unsure,
but my heart said, "You're prepared."
I thought about my goal-filled rocket,
and took a breath of steady air.

I passed the launch test with a smile.
I fixed the panel, steered with grace.
My crew all cheered, and I just grinned—
I'd earned my journey into space.

Now I'm not afraid to fail.
Each step I take helps me grow strong.
My dreams once felt so far away—
but now I know I do belong.

So if you doubt what you can do,
just use the steps that helped me go:
Picture, Practice, Put goals down–
that's The Confidence Code, you know!

My Goal Rocket

My BIG Goal:

Step 1:
Picture yourself succeeding.

The End

Check out the fun Astronaut Ninja lesson plans at ninjalifehacks.tv

I love to hear from my readers. Email me your feedback or thoughts on what my next story should be at info@ninjalifehacks.tv   Yours truly, Mary

 @marynhin   @officialninjalifehacks
#NinjaLifeHacks

 Ninja Life Hacks

 Mary Nhin   Ninja Life Hacks

 @officialninjalifehacks

Build Your Own Goal Rocket!

Your Mission:

Just like Astronaut Ninja, you're about to launch into greatness! Follow these 3 steps of the Confidence Code:

1. Picture Yourself Succeeding:
Draw a picture of you achieving your big dream. Are you an inventor? A teacher? A space explorer?

Draw it here:

2. Practice Failing:
Write or draw a time you made a mistake but kept going. What did you learn?

3. Put Your Goals on a Rocket:
Write 3 big goals you have. Then draw them on your very own rocket below!

Goal #1: _____
Goal #2: _____
Goal #3: _____

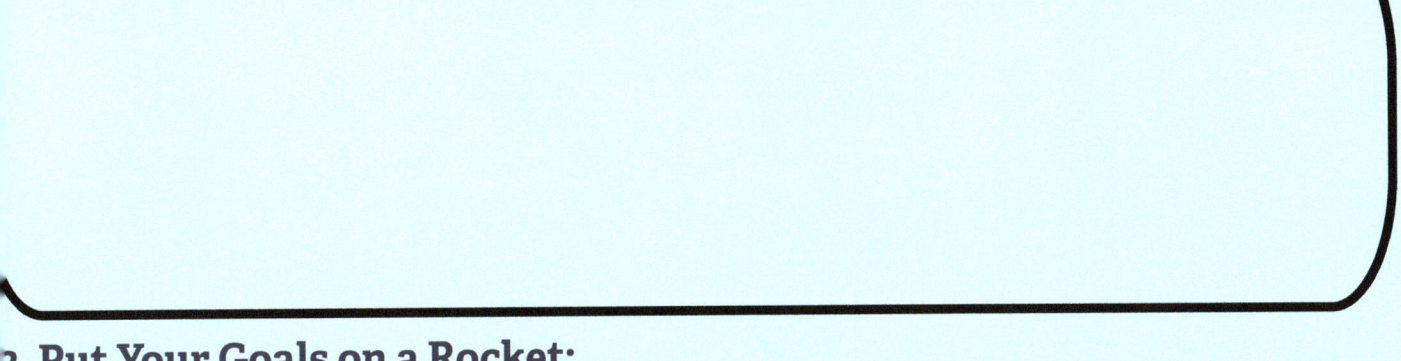